the
vegetarian
cookbook

DK

DK | Penguin Random House

Senior editor Carrie Love
US Senior editor Shannon Beatty
US editor Margaret Parrish
Senior designer Rachael Parfitt Hunt
Designers Eleanor Bates, Rachael Hare, Karen Hood, Hannah Moore
Editorial assistant Becky Walsh
Recipe writers Heather Whinney and Denise Smart
Nutritionist Fiona Hunter
US Consultant Kate Curnes
Food stylist Denise Smart
Photographer Dave King
Pre-production producers Sophie Chatellier and Jennifer Murray
Producer John Casey
Jacket designers Sonny Flynn and Rachael Parfitt Hunt
Jacket coordinator Issy Walsh
Managing editor Penny Smith
Managing art editor Mabel Chan
Creative director Helen Senior
Publishing director Sarah Larter

First American Edition, 2019
Published in the United States by DK Publishing
1450 Broadway, Suite 801, New York, New York 10018

Contents

Best breakfasts

Super snacks

Lovely lunches

Delicious drinks

Enticing entrées

Sweet stuff

Kitchen rules

Cooking is meant to be fun and a little bit messy, but you still need to keep safety and cleanliness in mind. Follow instructions carefully, gather everything together, and read through these rules and tips before you begin.

INGREDIENTS AND EQUIPMENT

• Make sure you have all your ingredients laid out before you start to make a recipe. You'll probably have most ingredients in your kitchen already, but some you will need to buy.

• Always use the type of flour specified in a recipe—bread, all-purpose, or self-rising.

• Use medium-sized free-range eggs unless stated otherwise.

• For recipes that require milk, you can use whole, low-fat, skim, or plant-based milk. For cheese, use vegan or dairy cheese. Choose a dairy cheese that isn't made with rennet.

Preheating the oven
Follow the temperature instructions within each recipe.

Special equipment
Keep an eye out for recipes that require special equipment. Buy or borrow items in advance if you don't own them.

WEIGHTS AND MEASUREMENTS

Carefully measure the ingredients before you start a recipe. Use measuring spoons, weighing scales, and a measuring cup, as necessary. Below are the abbreviations and full names for the measurements used in this book.

Metric	US measures	Spoon measures
g = gram	oz = ounce	tsp = teaspoon
ml = milliliter	lb = pound	tbsp = tablespoon
cm = centimeter	fl oz = fluid ounce	
	in = inch	

GETTING STARTED

1

Read a recipe all the way through before you start.

2

Wash your hands, put on an apron, and tie back your hair.

3

Make sure you have all the ingredients and equipment on hand before you begin cooking.

KITCHEN SAFETY

Be very careful...

• Around hot ovens, and gas or electric stoves, making sure you know whether the oven or stove is on (and off), and protecting your hands when touching or lifting anything hot from, or on, or into it. Oven mitts are your friends here!

• Handling hot liquids or hot pans, watching carefully for spills, and protecting your hands (using oven mitts or a dish towel) when moving or holding hot items. Use a spatter screen when cooking with hot oil. Tell an adult immediately if you get a burn.

• Handling anything sharp, such as knives or a grater. Take extra care when cutting a large fruit or vegetable that has a thick or hard peel, such as a watermelon, pumpkin, or butternut squash. Cut it into quarters first to make the task safer. Then cut off the peel before chopping the flesh into chunks.

• Using electric tools, such as blenders, food processors, mixers, and microwaves. Check if they're on, and don't put your hands near the moving parts until they are unplugged.

• Always wash your hands thoroughly after handling chile peppers, jalapeños, and chile flakes, and avoid touching your eyes, mouth or other sensitive areas.

IF IN DOUBT, ask an ADULT to help, especially when you're unsure about anything.

MAKES/SERVES

This lists the amount of portions a recipe makes or how many people it serves.

PREP/CHILL/REST/ SOAK/RISE/PROOF/ CHURN/FREEZE

This tells you how many minutes and hours a recipe will take to prepare. It includes specific times for extra preparation, such as chilling and rising. Remember that preparation times might take a little longer if it's the first time you're making a recipe.

COOK

This tells you how long it will take to cook a dish.

KITCHEN HYGIENE

When you're in the kitchen, follow these important rules to keep germs in check.

• Always wash your hands before you start any recipe.

• Wash all fruits and vegetables.

• Use hot, soapy water to clean cutting boards after using them.

• Store raw and cooked food separately.

• Keep your cooking area clean and have a cloth handy to mop up any spills.

• Always check the use-by date on all ingredients.

• Wash your hands after handling raw eggs. Hollandaise sauce and Zingy lime pie have egg that isn't fully cooked, so don't serve this to a baby, an elderly person, or a pregnant woman.

Equipment

This handy guide features all the special equipment used in this book. Make sure you have the right equipment ready before cooking.

Cups

Small bowls

Glasses

Grater

Electric mixer

Ladle

Slotted spoon

Masher

Serrated knife

Sharp knives

Pizza cutter

Basting brush

Peeler

Garlic press

Whisks

Kitchen scissors

Ice cream scoop

Splatter screen

Muffin pan and paper liners

Colander

Sieve

Cutting board

Pie pan

Oven dish

Baking pan

Baking pans, Baking sheet

Stand mixer

Wire rack

Piping bag and nozzles

Measuring spoons

Measuring cups

Blender, Food processor

Glass pitcher

Pizza dish

Flour shaker

Bamboo steamer

Paper straws

Measuring cup

Cocktail shaker

Zester

Muddler

Juicer

Glass bowls

Large bowl

Chopsticks

Plastic spatulas

Wooden spoon

Wooden spatulas

Spoons

Butter knife

Fork

Skewers

Cocktail sticks

Rolling pin

Foil

Parchment paper

Plastic wrap

Grill pan

Milk pan

Heavy-bottomed saucepan

Frying pans

Large saucepan

Wok

Plastic gloves

Oven mitts

7

Healthy eating

The secret to a healthy vegetarian diet is balance. Your body needs more than 40 different nutrients to keep it healthy. This circle shows the proportion of food you need to eat from each food group. No single food provides all the nutrients your body needs, so it's important to eat a variety of different types of food every day.

Fruits and vegetables

These provide vitamins, minerals, phytochemicals (a chemical compound found in plants), and fiber. You need to eat at least five servings a day.

Water

It's not just the food on your plate that's important. You need to drink between 6-8 glasses of fluid a day—water is the healthiest choice.

Proteins

Beans, nuts, and seeds are a vital source of protein, which is essential for the growth and repair of cells in your body.

Fruits and vegetables

Proteins

Potatoes, bread, rice, pasta, and other starchy carbohydrates

To help you get the right balance and all the nutrients you need, nutritionists divide food into different groups. You don't need to eat the exact balance of nutrients at every meal, but you should try to get the right balance daily, as shown, as often as you can.

Eat up!

Did you know?

Amino acids are the building blocks that make up protein. The body cannot make some of them, so they need to be provided by the food you eat.

Potatoes, bread, rice, pasta, and other starchy carbohydrates

Bread, cereal, potatoes, rice, pasta, and grains are high in carbohydrates, which gives your body energy. Whole grain options, like whole wheat bread, are the healthiest choice.

Oils and spreads

Fat is found in oils and spreads. It is essential in your diet, but don't eat too much of it and choose healthy fats, such as avocados and olive oil.

Dairy

Foods such as milk, cheese, and yogurt provide calcium, which helps give us strong bones and teeth. They also contain protein, vitamins A, B2, and B12.

Parsnips

They are a good source of fiber and also provide you with the B vitamin called folate.

Carrots

As an excellent source of vitamin A, carrots help to keep your skin and eyes healthy.

Arugula

Deep green salad leaves, such as arugula, contain more vitamins than lighter leaves.

Celery

Due to its high water content, celery can help keep you hydrated. It's also rich in vitamins A, C, and K.

Vegetables

Try to eat a variety of veggies to get lots of different nutrients. Some of the foods on these pages are actually fruits, but are sold as vegetables.

Mushrooms

Just three handfuls of sliced mushrooms count as one of your five-a-day.

Onions

The fiber in onions encourages friendly bacteria to grow in your gut.

Broccoli

This is an excellent source of vitamins C and K, as well as the B vitamin folate.

Kale

These tasty leaves are rich in vitamins A, C, and K, as well as phytochemicals, which help to keep your eyes healthy.

Spinach

Packed with folate, vitamin C, and potassium, spinach helps to keep your blood, immune system, and eyes healthy.

Cauliflower

Rich in vitamin K, cauliflower helps to keep your bones healthy.

Beets

These are rich in folate, which helps your body make red blood cells and keeps your immune system healthy.

Bell peppers

Bell peppers are a fruit. All bell peppers are superrich in vitamins A and C. Half of a red bell pepper contains more vitamin C than an orange.

Butternut squash

These are a fruit. They're rich in phytochemicals, called carotenoids, which can help make your skin look healthier.

Peas

Peas are a useful source of iron for vegetarians.

Sweet potatoes

Unlike regular white potatoes, sweet potatoes count toward your five-a-day target.

Cucumbers

Cucumber is a fruit. Just a 2in (5cm) piece of cucumber counts as one of your five-a-day.

Pumpkins

Pumpkins are a fruit. They're a great source of betacarotene, which the body can use to make vitamin A.

Watermelons
These are rich in vitamin B6, which you need for a healthy immune system.

Oranges
Superrich in vitamin C, oranges are also a good source of the B vitamins called B1 and folate.

Figs
Fresh and dried figs are rich in fiber and make a healthy snack.

Fruits
Fruits comes in a rainbow of colors. Each one has a distinct nutritional profile. Try eating a variety of colors every week.

Mangoes
These are rich in betacarotene, which helps to keep your skin and eyes healthy.

Raisins
Rich in fiber, these are a delicious treat, but limit the amount you eat as they are very high in sugar.

Avocados
These are packed with vitamins E and B6, as well as healthy fats and fiber.

Lemons
Packed with vitamin C, lemons help the body to use iron from other foods.

Peaches
You will get around half the recommended daily amount of vitamin C from one medium peach.

Apples
As a good source of fiber, apples help to keep your digestive system healthy.

Limes
If you add lime or lemon juice to flavor your food, you won't need as much salt.

Tomatoes
These are actually a fruit, not a vegetable! There are more than 5,000 varieties.

Blueberries
These are full of phytochemicals, which help to keep your eyes, brain, and heart healthy.

Pineapples
These are a great source of fiber and vitamin C.

Raspberries
Raspberries are rich in manganese and vitamin K, which both play a role in bone health.

Strawberries
These are rich in vitamin C and the B vitamin folate.

Apricots
These contain betacarotene, which your body can convert into vitamin A.

Kiwis
These contain a phytochemical called lutein, which keeps your eyes healthy.

13

Rice

Brown rice contains three times more fiber than white rice.

Pita breads

These are excellent toasted and eaten with dips. They are a quick and easy source of energy.

Starchy carbohydrates

Try to include these great sources of carbohydrate at every meal—high fiber or whole grain varieties are best. Carbs give your body energy.

Oats

Oats are a great choice for breakfast, because they release energy slowly over the morning.

Barley

Barley is higher in fiber than white, brown, and wild rice.

Breads

Bread gives your body energy. Whole grain varieties are highest in vitamins, minerals, and fiber.

Pasta

Pasta can be eaten hot, or cold in salads. Whole grain pasta is best for you.

Noodles
There are many types of noodles. If you don't eat eggs, choose rice noodles instead, which are also gluten free.

Quinoa
This healthy seed contains three times more iron than brown rice.

Tortilla wraps
These are filling and make an easy lunch. Choose whole wheat varieties.

Potatoes
Rich in vitamin C and potassium, potatoes also contain fiber, which is mostly found in the skin.

Whole wheat flour
This contains more fiber and B vitamins than white flour.

Sweet potatoes
Delicious roasted, mashed, or served as wedges, sweet potatoes are a good source of vitamins A and C.

Couscous
This can be eaten hot or cold—choose whole grain couscous whenever you can.

Bulgur wheat
This is a good alternative to couscous, because it releases energy more slowly.

Halloumi cheese
Unlike other cheese, halloumi doesn't melt when it's heated. It is good served alongside roasted vegetables.

Plain yogurt
A ⅔ cup serving of yogurt provides a quarter of your daily calcium intake and almost half of your daily iodine needs.

Vegetarian hard cheese
Use this instead of Parmesan cheese.

Milk
As well as calcium, milk is a source of protein, iodine, vitamins A, B2, B12, and D.

Vegetarian cheese
Some cheeses are made with enzymes from the inside of a cow's stomach, called rennet. For true vegetarian cheese, look for cheese made without rennet or with non-animal rennet.

Feta cheese
This cheese is high in salt, so use it sparingly!

Dairy

Dairy is rich in calcium, which makes your bones strong. If you don't eat dairy, make sure you eat other calcium-rich foods.

Cheddar cheese
This is a good source of vitamins A, B12, and the minerals calcium and phosphorus.

Smoothies
Ready-made smoothies can contain added sugar, so it's best to make your own by blending fresh fruit with milk or yogurt.

Plant milk
If you choose a plant-based milk instead of cow's milk, choose one that has calcium and vitamin D added.

Flavorings

Basil

These aromatic leaves add flavor to many Italian dishes and are used to make pesto.

Cilantro

It's used in lots of Mexican dishes. It tastes great in dips and salads.

Mint

These refreshing leaves are very versatile—add them to a drink or eat with veggies.

Chives

Snip these lightly onion-flavored stems into yogurt dips, salads, or soups.

Parsley

Stir or sprinkle these leaves into casseroles or rice dishes. They add a fresh flavor.

Bay leaf
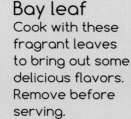
Cook with these fragrant leaves to bring out some delicious flavors. Remove before serving.

Turmeric

This strongly scented, bright yellow spice is often used in Indian cooking.

Paprika

This rich spice has a mild chile flavor that enhances lots of dishes.

Cumin
Add a pinch of this warming, pungent spice to your curry to add extra flavor.

Chile flakes
At the start of cooking, add a sprinkle of chile flakes to give a fiery flavor to your dish.

Salt
A pinch of salt will enhance the flavor of your food. Ensure you use it sparingly.

Black pepper
Freshly ground black pepper adds a depth of flavor to any savory dish.

Vinegar
Mix a splash with olive oil to make a salad dressing with a kick.

Lemon
A squeeze of tangy lemon juice over food provides vitamin C.

Lime
This sharp, zingy citrus flavor goes well with spicy dishes.

Star anise
This spice has a light licorice flavor. Always remove star anise before serving.

Cinnamon
Cinnamon sticks can be used in both savory and sweet dishes.

Garlic

Cook with onions to add a punchy flavor to all savory dishes.

Ginger

A zesty spice used in Asian cooking—it's super tasty in a stir-fry.

Pumpkin seeds
In addition to protein, these are a good source of zinc.

Almonds
These are rich in calcium, which is very important if you don't eat dairy.

Cheese
All types of cheese are rich in protein, but they also provide B vitamins and calcium.

Proteins
Lots of foods provide protein. Eating a variety of foods from this group will help you get your essential amino acids.

Pistachios
In addition to protein, all nuts provide healthy fats.

Peanut butter
In addition to protein, peanut butter is a good source of healthy fat.

Beans
All beans are packed with protein. Just three heaping tablespoons count as one of your five-a-day.

Cashews
Cashews are rich in zinc and vitamins E and K. When blended, they make a creamy base for dips and dressings.

18

Chickpeas

Canned chickpeas are quick and easy to use, and just as nutritious as dried ones, which require more time to prepare. Just make sure you rinse them first!

Milk

This provides protein in your diet, but is also a good source of calcium, which is important for healthy bones.

Pine nuts

These contain protein and vitamin E. They also contain vitamin K, which helps keep blood healthy.

Lentils

In addition to being high in protein, lentils are rich in fiber and B vitamins.

Eggs

On top of protein, eggs contain other nutrients, including vitamins B12 and D, as well as iodine.

Fiber

Fruits and veggies

Fresh, frozen, and dried fruit all provide good amounts of fiber. All vegetables provide fiber.

Oats

These contain a type of fiber that helps to keep your heart and digestive system healthy.

Whole grain food

Whole grains contain more fiber, vitamins, and minerals than "white" carbs.

Beans

All beans, including baked beans, and hummus, which is made from chickpeas, are a good source of fiber.

Nuts and seeds

All nut and seed products, like nut butters, are also rich in fiber.

Potatoes

Most of the fiber in potatoes is found in the skin, so try eating potatoes with the skin on.

Best breakfasts

Dig in!

Whether you're a morning person or not, it's important to eat a nutritious breakfast to set you up for the day. Wake up to tasty Swiss oatmeal, make a simple avocado on toast, flip pancakes with a veggie twist, or cook absolutely perfect eggs!

Avocado on sourdough toast

Creamy, mashed avocado is a filling and tasty start to any morning. It's really easy and quick to make. Leave out the chile flakes if you're not into spicy food.

chile flakes

In a large bowl, add the avocado, lemon juice, and chia seeds. Season well with the salt and pepper. Gently mash the ingredients with the back of a fork. Spread the mixture over the warm toast. Sprinkle the cilantro and chile flakes on top, if using.

salt and pepper

cilantro

sourdough bread

Ingredients

2 avocados, halved
and pitted

juice of 1 lemon

2 tsp chia seeds

sea salt and freshly ground
black pepper

4 chunky slices of sourdough
bread, toasted

handful of cilantro

sprinkle of chile flakes
(optional)

avocado

lemon

chia seeds

23

Scrambled eggs

Once you've mastered this delicious recipe you can start to add other flavors and ingredients to make your perfect eggs.

Ingredients

2 tbsp butter

2 eggs

¼ cup milk

sea salt and freshly ground black pepper

4 slices of multi grain bread, toasted and buttered, to serve

2 tsp chives, chopped, to serve (optional)

SERVES 2
PREP 5 MINS
COOK 5 MINS

1

Heat the butter in a nonstick frying pan until just foaming. In a bowl, lightly whisk the eggs and milk together. Season well.

2

Pour the mixture into the pan and leave it for a few seconds. Using a wooden spoon, begin to fold it over and stir gently. Leave to set, then gently fold over again.

Try this

Once the eggs are cooked, stir in a handful of chopped fresh tomatoes or a few cooked mushrooms. You can also add a sprinkling of grated cheese.

3

Remove the pan from the heat just before the eggs are cooked—they should still be wet and wobbly. The eggs will continue to cook in the pan for another minute. Stir again; serve on the toast. Sprinkle with chives, if using.

stir it!

Mango yogurt with
toast dippers

This is a simple and healthy way to start the day—the juicy mango is delicious with yogurt. You can sweeten it with a drizzle of honey and toasted coconut, if you like.

yogurt

Spoon a little yogurt into two bowls, then add the chopped mango. Sprinkle with toasted coconut and drizzle with honey, if using. Slice the brioche into fingers and serve with the yogurt.

coconut

brioche

Ingredients

1 cup plain Greek yogurt

1 mango, halved, pitted, and chopped

2 slices of brioche (or other bread), lightly toasted

2 small pieces of fresh coconut, sliced and toasted (optional)

drizzle of honey (optional)

honey

mango

27

Crunchy, sweet pancakes

These yummy pancakes have all the flavors of a carrot cake! They are perfect for breakfast or lunch—and even sweet enough to have for dessert!

MAKES 12
PREP 12 MINS
COOK 15 MINS

1 Add the flour, baking powder, salt, sugar, and cinnamon to a large bowl and mix together.

2 In another bowl, whisk the eggs and milk together. Pour the egg mixture into the flour mixture. Beat to form a batter.

3 Add the grated carrot and raisins to the mixture. Gently fold in until evenly distributed.

Ingredients

1¼ cups all-purpose flour

2 tsp baking powder

pinch of sea salt

2 tbsp granulated sugar

1 tsp ground cinnamon

3 eggs

⅔ cup whole milk

2 carrots, grated and squeezed to remove water

handful of raisins

vegetable oil, for frying

drizzle of maple syrup, to serve

4 Heat a drizzle of oil in a nonstick frying pan. When hot, add a dollop of batter to the pan. You should be able to cook three pancakes at a time.

5 Cook for 2-3 minutes, then flip using a spatula and cook the other side for another 2-3 minutes. Move to a plate and cook the remaining pancakes. Serve with a drizzle of maple syrup.

golden brown

29

Swiss oatmeal

This sweet breakfast treat starts with oats soaked overnight in apple juice. Add a delicious mix of fruits and nuts and it's a tasty way to start the day!

milk

raspberries

In a large bowl, combine the oats, dried fruits, and apple juice. Let soak overnight. In another bowl, mix the grated apple and milk, then stir the mix into the soaked oats and fruit. Sprinkle the nuts and a spoonful of yogurt on top. Add the raspberries and drizzle with honey.

apricots

figs

yogurt

honey

Ingredients

½ cup rolled oats

2 tbsp dried apricots, chopped

2 tbsp dried figs, chopped

⅔ cup apple juice

1 apple, grated

splash of milk

handful of almonds, coarsely chopped

1 heaping tbsp plain Greek yogurt, to serve

handful of raspberries, to serve

honey, to serve

oats

almonds

apple juice

grated apple

31

Poached eggs with greens and hollandaise sauce

Served with the lemony, buttery hollandaise sauce, poached eggs are a great dish for a weekend breakfast.

SERVES 2
PREP 15 MINS
COOK 20 MINS

1 For the hollandaise sauce, melt the butter in a small pan and set aside.

2

In a heatproof bowl, add the egg yolk, vinegar, salt, and a sprinkle of ice-cold water. Put the bowl over a pan of simmering water. Whisk until the sauce starts to thicken. Take off the heat, whisk in the butter, and add the lemon juice. Set aside.

Ingredients

For the hollandaise sauce

9 tbsp butter

1 egg yolk

¼ tsp white balsamic vinegar

pinch of sea salt

squeeze of lemon juice

For the poached eggs

7oz (200g) spinach leaves or Swiss chard

2 eggs

4 slices of English muffin, toasted

pinch of paprika

* Please note: the hollandaise sauce contains egg that isn't fully cooked.

3

Steam the spinach or Swiss chard in a metal colander over a pan of simmering water. Season with salt. Cover, and cook for 2 minutes, or until tender. Set aside and keep warm.

4

Crack an egg into a cup. Boil a pan of water and swirl it with a spoon to make a gentle whirlpool. Slowly pour the egg into the center of the whirlpool. Cook for 3–4 minutes, until the white is cooked. Use a slotted spoon to remove the eggs.

5 Put the greens on the muffin slices and top with an egg. Drizzle the sauce over the top. Sprinkle with paprika and serve.

Super
snacks

When you're hungry for a snack, reach for tasty cheesy muffins and fresh salad bowls. Then, dip into delicious flatbreads, sweet potato fries, homemade nachos, sliced veggies, plantain chips, and Chinese rolls!

Flatbreads
and dips

Make one or all of these yummy dips to serve with the flatbreads. Which one is your favorite?

MAKES **6**
PREP **25 MINS**
COOK **25 MINS**

Ingredients

- 1¼ cups self-rising flour, plus extra for dusting
- 1 tsp baking powder
- ¾ cup plain yogurt

1

In a large bowl, add the flour, baking powder, and yogurt.

2

Using your hands, bring everything together to form a dough.

3

Turn the dough onto a lightly floured surface and knead for a few minutes.

4

Put the dough in a bowl and leave for 15 minutes. Carefully cut it in half, then cut each half into three, and roll into balls. On a lightly floured surface, roll each ball into a 4in (10cm) round.

5

One at a time, carefully put the rounds in a hot grill pan and cook for 2 minutes on each side, until golden. Serve warm with the dips.

Blend!

mix well

Puree!

Cashew dip

Soak 1 cup cashews in water for 2 hours. Blend ½ cup extra virgin olive oil, 2 garlic cloves, 1 tbsp balsamic vinegar, seasoning, and the cashews in a food processor. Add a little water if needed. Top with snipped chives to serve.

Baba ganoush

Prick 2 eggplants all over with a fork, then broil for 15 minutes, until tender. When cool, remove the skin and put the flesh in a bowl with 2 mashed garlic cloves, 1-2 tbsp tahini, juice of ½ lemon, 2 tbsp extra virgin olive oil, and seasoning. Mix well.

Red pepper hummus

Add a drained 12oz (350g) jar of roasted red peppers, 2 x 14oz (400g) cans of rinsed and drained chickpeas, 2-3 tbsp extra virgin olive oil, pinch of ground cumin, 2 garlic cloves, and seasoning to a food processor and blend. Add a little water if needed.

Plantain chips **and dips**

This is an easy snack to make ahead and then enjoy with your friends.

SERVES 4
PREP 15 MINS
COOK 20 MINS

Ingredients

2 green plantains, or unripe green bananas

2 tsp extra virgin olive oil

salt and freshly ground black pepper

1

Preheat the oven to 400°F (200°C). Peel the plantains or bananas and thinly slice them carefully.

2

Coat it!

Line a baking sheet with parchment paper. In a bowl, coat the plantains in the oil and season. Place on the sheet.

3

Bake for 20 minutes, or until golden. The chips should just be beginning to crisp. Transfer to a bowl and serve with the dips.

Mix it!

lemon juice

paprika

Garlic and lemon yogurt dip

In a bowl, mix together 1 cup plain Greek yogurt, juice of 1 lemon, pinch of sea salt, pinch of paprika, and 3 garlic cloves, mashed. Spoon into a serving dish. Top with a few gratings of lemon zest.

red chiles

lime juice

Lime and chile mayonnaise dip

In a bowl, mix together juice of 1 lime, 1 tsp paprika, 6 tbsp mayonnaise, and 1 chile, finely chopped. Season with black pepper and salt. Spoon into a serving dish. Dust with another 1 tsp paprika.

Warm and fruity
bulgur wheat salad

This colorful, hot-grain salad with Moroccan spices is a super easy dish to make ahead.

SERVES 4
PREP 15 MINS
COOK 10 MINS

1

Put the bulgur wheat and a pinch of salt in a pan. Pour in boiling water about 2in (5cm) above the bulgur. Cover and simmer gently for 5-6 minutes. Turn off the heat and let steam a little. Uncover and use a fork to fluff up the bulgur. Move to a large bowl.

Stir!

2

Heat the oil in a pan, add the onion and spices. Season well. Cook for 2-3 minutes, then stir in the garlic and bell peppers. Cook a few minutes more, until the peppers are softened. Add to the bulgur wheat and stir.

Ingredients

10oz (300g) bulgur wheat

sea salt and freshly ground black pepper

1 tbsp olive oil

1 red onion, finely chopped

pinch of ground cinnamon

pinch of ground cumin

2 garlic cloves, finely chopped

1 red bell pepper and 1 yellow bell pepper, halved, seeded, and finely chopped

14oz (400g) can chickpeas, rinsed, drained, and cooked carefully in boiling water for 4 minutes

handful of raisins

handful of shelled, raw pistachios, chopped

bunch of cilantro, chopped

bunch of mint, chopped

2 oranges, chopped into bite-size pieces

For the dressing

3 tbsp extra virgin olive oil

1 tbsp white balsamic vinegar

sea salt and freshly ground black pepper

3

Add the chickpeas, raisins, pistachios, and herbs and stir well. Season again, if needed.

4

Stir in the dressing, then lightly stir in the orange pieces. Serve warm.

Mix it!

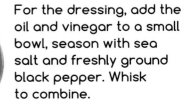

For the dressing, add the oil and vinegar to a small bowl, season with sea salt and freshly ground black pepper. Whisk to combine.

Summer
rolls

These are really simple to make as you do not need to cook these fresh summer rolls. You can be as adventurous as you like with the filling.

Fill a large bowl with cold water and add the rice paper wrappers one at a time.

Pat with your hands until they start to feel just pliable; don't soak too long or they will tear. Place the paper wrappers on a damp, clean dish towel.

Top a rice paper wrapper with a few greens. Add bell peppers, bean sprouts, carrots, scallions, and cucumber. Finish with a few herbs.

Ingredients

24 rice paper wrappers, about 8½in (22cm) in diameter

large handful of mixed greens

7oz (200g) bean sprouts

2 red bell peppers, seeded and sliced into fine strips

2 carrots, peeled and sliced into fine strips

bunch of scallions, trimmed, halved, and finely sliced lengthwise

1 cucumber, halved lengthwise, seeds removed, and sliced into fine strips

handful of fresh basil leaves

handful of fresh mint leaves

For the dipping sauce

¼ cup dark soy sauce

2 garlic cloves, finely chopped

1 small red chile, finely chopped

1 tbsp finely chopped ginger

2 tsp granulated sugar

juice of 1 lime

Bring the bottom of the wrapper up over the filling and roll tightly.

Fold the edges in and continue rolling until the roll is tight. Repeat with the remaining wrappers.

Add all the ingredients for the dipping sauce into a bowl, mix well, and serve with the rolls. When ready to serve, carefully slice each roll in half at an angle and arrange on a large plate with the dipping sauce.

Crudités
and dips

Crudités are raw veggies, and this is an easy, fun way to eat up your five-a-day. Be as adventurous as you want with your choice of vegetables—if it's good eaten raw, chop it and add it to the mix.

Spoon the dips into individual serving bowls, put them on a large platter or board, and serve with the crudités.

bell
pepper

In a bowl, mix ¾ cup sour cream, a splash of milk, 1 tsp balsamic vinegar, and a small handful of chopped chives, dill, and parsley. Season with sea salt and freshly ground black pepper.

celery

Sour cream
and herb dip

Yogurt and feta dip

In a bowl, beat together 1 cup plain Greek yogurt with 7oz (200g) feta cheese. Mix in the juice of ½ lemon, a sprinkle of chile flakes, and season with freshly ground black pepper.

Ingredients

3 carrots, peeled and cut into baton shapes

3 bell peppers, a mix of red, yellow, and orange, seeded and cut into strips

several celery stalks, trimmed and cut into baton shapes

handful of sugar snap peas

1 cucumber, seeded and cut into baton shapes

cucumber

carrot

Add a 10oz (300g) package cooked beets to a food processor and puree. Add ¼ cup crème fraîche or plain yogurt, a pinch of sumac, a small handful of mint leaves, and season well with sea salt and freshly ground black pepper. Puree until smooth.

Beet and mint dip

sugar snap peas

Homemade
nachos

SERVES 6
PREP 15 MINS
COOK 10 MINS

This sharing platter of homemade nachos, piled high with beans, salsa, and melted cheese, is perfect for a get-together.

Did you know?
Each portion of this dish will provide two servings of vegetables and almost one-third of the total amount of fiber you need each day!

1

Preheat the oven to 400°F (200°C). Lightly brush a large baking sheet with the oil. Add the tortilla triangles and sprinkle with paprika. Put in the oven and bake for about 4–5 minutes, or until golden.

2

Mix the avocado in a bowl with the lemon juice.

3

Spoon the warmed refried beans, avocado, and jalapeños (if using) on top. Sprinkle with grated cheese. Return to the oven. Bake for a few minutes, until the cheese is melted.

cheese

avocado

refried beans

4

Top with the salsa, a dollop of sour cream, and scatter cilantro on top, if using. Serve with lime wedges.

Ingredients

½ tbsp olive oil, plus extra for brushing

12 whole wheat tortillas, sliced into triangles

pinch of paprika

2 avocados, pitted and coarsely chopped

juice of ½ lemon

14oz (400g) can refried beans, gently heated

1 jalapeño, sliced (depending on how hot you like it)

5½oz (150g) cheese, grated

¾ cup sour cream, to serve

a few cilantro leaves to garnish (optional)

lime wedges, to serve

For the salsa

8 tomatoes, finely diced

1 small onion, diced

2 cloves garlic, finely chopped

1 red chile, halved, seeded, and finely chopped

large handful of cilantro, chopped

juice of ½ lime

2–3 tsp balsamic vinegar

sea salt and freshly ground black pepper

cilantro

tomato

In a bowl, combine the ingredients for the salsa.

red chile

garlic

onion

Cheese and herb muffins

If you are new to baking, these muffins are a good place to start. They're super easy to make and wonderfully tasty.

1

Preheat the oven to 400°F (200°C). Line 10 holes in the muffin pan with the paper liners. In a bowl, combine the flour, baking powder, and most of the cheese.

2

Put the spinach in a bowl, cover with plastic wrap, and microwave for 3 minutes. Once cool, chop finely. Add the spinach, butter, milk, eggs, and chives to a bowl. Season well.

3

Add the wet mixture to the dry mixture and beat it all together with a wooden spoon. Don't worry about lumps—these will disappear while the muffins bake.

Ingredients

1 cup self-rising flour

1 tsp baking powder

5½oz (150g) cheddar cheese, grated

3½oz (100g) baby spinach leaves

2 tbsp butter, melted

½ cup milk

2 eggs

handful of chives, finely chopped

sea salt and freshly ground black pepper

Special equipment

12-hole muffin pan

10 paper liners

4

Bake!

Spoon the mixture into the paper liners, sprinkle the remaining cheese on top, and bake for 18–20 minutes, until the muffins are risen and baked through. They are delicious when eaten warm!

Watermelon and feta
summer salad

Whip up this sweet and salty dish on a hot summer day. Serve it as a snack or a light lunch.

feta cheese

pine nuts

Toss it!

In a large salad bowl, gently toss the watermelon, red onion, feta, black-eyed peas, basil, and two-thirds of the pine nuts.

In another bowl, mix the oil and lemon juice for the dressing. Season with black pepper. Drizzle on the salad. Top with the remaining pine nuts.

50

basil leaves

red onion

Ingredients

½ small watermelon, peeled carefully cut into quarters, seeded, and chopped

½ small red onion, thinly sliced

4½oz (125g) feta cheese, crumbled

15oz (420g) can black-eyed peas in water, rinsed and drained

large handful of basil leaves, coarsely torn

¼ cup pine nuts

For the dressing

2 tsp olive oil

juice of ½ lemon

freshly ground black pepper

black-eyed peas

watermelon

Parsnip and
sweet potato fries

Switch regular potato fries for a sweeter and more nutritious version. They are great served on their own or as a side to a main meal.

Ingredients

14oz (400g) parsnips, peeled

14oz (400g) sweet potatoes, peeled

2 tbsp olive oil

2 garlic cloves, crushed

pinch of paprika

pinch of sea salt and freshly ground black pepper

ketchup, to serve

mayonnaise, to serve

chop it!

Make the fries thick or thin.

SERVES 4
PREP 15 MINS
COOK 30 MINS

1 Preheat the oven to 400°F (200°C). Carefully chop the parsnips and sweet potatoes into fry shapes.

2

Place the fries in a large bowl, then add the oil, garlic, paprika, and seasoning. Toss together.

3

Put the fries on a baking sheet and bake in the oven for 20–30 minutes, until golden. Keep an eye on them, as they can burn quickly. Serve warm with ketchup and mayonnaise.

Lovely lunches

Dip in!

Feast on these tasty dishes from around the world—from Mexican veggie wraps and quesadillas, to Italian frittata, risotto, and pasta pesto! They're filling and full of flavor and loaded with energy to keep you going all afternoon.

Vegetable wraps

Everyone loves Mexican-style wraps, and this veggie version is packed with lots of flavor!

Ingredients

1 red onion, coarsely chopped

1 red bell pepper and 1 orange bell pepper, halved, seeded, and coarsely chopped

pinch of ground cumin

pinch of paprika

sea salt and freshly ground black pepper

2 tbsp olive oil

7oz (200g) halloumi, sliced

large handful of spring mix lettuce

4 large flour tortillas, warmed

2 tomatoes, chopped

1 tbsp chipotle sauce

¼ cup plain yogurt

2 limes, cut into wedges

handful of cilantro

For the guacamole

3 avocados, pitted and coarsely chopped

handful of cilantro

juice of ½ lime

1 tomato, finely chopped

SERVES 4
PREP 15 MINS
COOK 20 MINS

1

Preheat the oven to 400°F (200°C). Put the red onion and bell peppers in a roasting pan. Sprinkle with the cumin and paprika, season well, drizzle half the olive oil over the top and toss together. Roast in the oven for 20 minutes.

2

Meanwhile, toss the halloumi slices with the remaining oil. Heat a grill pan to hot and carefully add the slices a few at a time. Cook until char lines appear on the underside, then flip and cook the other side for a few seconds.

3

To assemble the wraps, put the greens down the middle of the tortillas. Add the roasted onions, bell peppers, tomatoes, and halloumi. Spoon on the chipotle sauce and guacamole. Add a spoonful of yogurt, a squeeze of lime juice, and a little cilantro. Do not overload or the wraps will be tricky to fold!

4

To fold, pull the top and bottom of the wrap over the filling.

Fold one half of the wrap over the filling, then pull the other half tightly over the top.

Turn the wrap over so that the folds are facedown. Serve immediately.

To make the guacamole, put the avocado, lime juice, cilantro, tomato, and some of the seasoning in a bowl. Mash and stir with a fork until you get a chunky mixture. Cover and refrigerate until ready to serve.

Pearl barley
risotto

SERVES 4
PREP 15 MINS
COOK 50 MINS

Risotto is usually made with risotto rice, but pearl barley makes this dish wonderfully chewy and nut-flavored.

Ask an adult to help you prepare the butternut squash. Be very careful when using a sharp knife. Carefully cut the vegetable into quarters before peeling/cutting the skin off. Then, seed and chop the flesh into chunks.

58

Ingredients

1 butternut squash, carefully peeled, seeded, and cubed

2 tbsp olive oil

salt and freshly ground black pepper

1 onion, finely chopped

2 garlic cloves, finely chopped

10oz (300g) pearl barley

1 vegetable stock cube, dissolved in 4 cups (1 liter) boiling water

handful of spinach leaves

handful of basil leaves, coarsely chopped

handful of pine nuts, roasted, or use unsalted, shelled pistachios, roasted

2 tbsp hard cheese, grated, to serve

1

Preheat the oven to 400°F (200°C). Put the squash in a roasting pan, drizzle half the oil over the top, season well, and toss to coat. Roast in the oven for 20–30 minutes, until tender.

2

In a large saucepan, heat the remaining oil. Add the onion, season, and cook for 2 minutes, until soft. Stir in the garlic and cook for 1 minute, then add the pearl barley and stir well.

3

Carefully add half of the vegetable stock, stir, and simmer for 5 minutes. Mix in the remaining stock, cover, and simmer for 30 minutes, until the pearl barley is tender.

4

Stir in the spinach until it wilts, then mix in the roasted squash, basil, and pine nuts. Serve with the grated cheese sprinkled on top.

Mix it!

Quesadillas

SERVES 4
PREP 15 MINS
COOK 45 MINS

Queso is Spanish for cheese, so that's one ingredient you'll definitely find in this twist on a Mexican quesadilla. This one is loaded with roasted sweet potato.

Did you know?

Beans are a great source of protein if you don't eat meat. Protein helps keep your body healthy and strong.

1

Preheat the oven to 400°F (200°C). Put the sweet potato in a roasting pan, drizzle a teaspoon of the olive oil on top, season well, and toss to coat. Roast in the oven for 20 minutes, or until tender.

2

Carefully heat the remaining oil in a frying pan over medium heat. Add the scallions and green chile, season well, and cook for 2 minutes. Add the black beans and the roasted sweet potato. Stir and heat through.

3

Heat another large frying pan on medium heat and carefully add a tortilla. Spread a quarter of the bean mixture on top. Add cheese and jalapeños, if using.

4

Top with another tortilla, press together, and cook for 3 minutes.

5 Carefully flip the quesadilla and cook the other side until golden. Remove from the pan with a spatula and slice into four triangles. Cook the remaining quesadillas. Serve with a dollop of slaw.

Ingredients

2 sweet potatoes, peeled and cubed

1 tbsp olive oil

salt and freshly ground black pepper

4 scallions, trimmed and finely chopped

1 green chile, seeded and finely chopped

14oz (400g) can black beans, rinsed and drained

8 flour or corn tortillas, warmed

large handful of cheddar cheese, grated

pickled jalapeño chiles, sliced (optional)

For the slaw

¼ green cabbage, finely chopped

1 carrot, grated

1 apple, grated

2 tbsp extra virgin olive oil

3 tbsp white balsamic vinegar

1 tbsp maple syrup

sprinkle of chile flakes (optional)

Stir it!

To make the slaw, put the cabbage, carrot, and apple into a large bowl. In a small bowl, mix the oil, vinegar, syrup, and chile flakes, if using. Season, then stir the mixture into the slaw.

Veggie
gyoza

Gyoza is the Japanese name for stuffed, half moon-shaped dumplings. These delicious steamed gyoza are super light and fluffy.

Ingredients

2 cups all-purpose flour, plus extra for dusting

7oz (200g) Napa cabbage

5½oz (150g) mushrooms

2 scallions

1 tbsp fresh ginger, grated

1 tbsp dark soy sauce

1 tbsp lime juice

½ egg, lightly beaten

sea salt and freshly ground black pepper

For the dipping sauce

2 tbsp dark soy sauce

2 tbsp lime juice

1 tsp granulated sugar

1 tsp fresh ginger, grated

Special equipment

steamer—a bamboo one is best, but not essential

1

For the dough, sift the flour into a large bowl. Slowly add ¾ cup warm water, mixing as you go, until the mixture forms a dough. You may not need all the water.

2

On a lightly floured surface, knead the dough for about 5 minutes, until smooth. Cover with a damp, clean dish towel and leave for 20 minutes.

3

For the filling, chop the cabbage, mushrooms, and scallions in a food processor. Place in a bowl. Mix in the ginger, soy sauce, lime juice, and egg. Season well.

4

Carefully cut the dough into three pieces. On a lightly floured surface, roll each piece into a sausage shape.

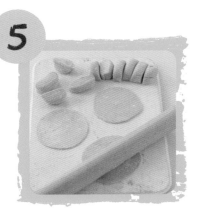

5

Carefully cut each sausage shape into 6 x ¾in (2cm) pieces. Roll each disk of dough into a circle 4in (10cm) wide.

6

Put a heaping teaspoon of filling in each circle. Dab water around the edges. Bring the edges together to form a pouch. Press to seal. Repeat with the rest of the dough and filling.

7

Line the steamer with parchment paper and place the dumplings in it. Put the steamer on a wok or large saucepan of boiling water. The water shouldn't touch the food. Cover and steam for about 8–10 minutes. Repeat in batches if you have a small steamer.

In a bowl, whisk together the ingredients for the dipping sauce and serve with the gyoza.

Pumpkin
soup

Perfect for lunch, this rich soup
is even better served with warm
toasted sourdough bread.

1

Carefully heat the oil in a large pan over medium heat. Add the onion, celery, and bay leaf. Season and cook for 2 minutes. Add the chopped garlic and ginger, then cook for another minute.

2

Stir in the pumpkin or squash and cook for 5 minutes, until it softens. Stir occasionally to prevent burning.

3

Carefully pour in the stock, and bring to a boil. Reduce to simmer. Cook for 15 minutes, or until tender.

Ingredients

1 tbsp olive oil

1 onion, finely chopped

2 celery stalks, finely chopped

1 bay leaf

pinch of sea salt and freshly ground black pepper

2 garlic cloves, finely chopped

1 tbsp fresh ginger, grated

2¼lb (1kg) pumpkin (or butternut squash), skin carefully peeled, flesh chopped into chunks, seeds reserved and roasted

1 vegetable stock cube, dissolved in 3 cups (750ml) boiling water

4 slices of sourdough bread, toasted, to serve

4

Remove the bay leaf. Carefully ladle the mixture into a blender and pulse until smooth. If the soup is too thick, add a little hot water. Pour into bowls and scatter the pumpkin seeds on top. Serve with the sourdough bread.

Ask an adult to help you prepare the pumpkin or butternut squash. Be very careful when using a sharp knife. Carefully cut the vegetable into quarters before peeling/ cutting the skin off. Then, seed and chop the flesh into chunks.

Puree!

65

Vegetable frittata

A frittata is an Italian omelet, and this one is filled with tasty veggies—you can add your own favorite veggies if you like.

Ingredients

1–2 tbsp olive oil

1 red onion, coarsely chopped

sea salt and freshly ground black pepper

½ butternut squash, carefully peeled, seeded, and cubed

5½oz (150g) mushrooms, sliced

large handful of kale leaves

large handful of spinach leaves

6 eggs

handful of grated hard cheese

1

Carefully heat the olive oil in a large nonstick frying pan over medium heat, then add the onion and season well. Cook for 3–4 minutes, until softened.

2

Stir in the butternut squash and cook for 8–10 minutes, or until softened. Add a little more oil if the squash starts to dry out. Be careful around hot oil.

3

Push the squash to one side of the pan and add the mushrooms. Cook for another 3 minutes.

4

Add the kale leaves and stir well. Cover and cook for 5 minutes, then add the spinach to the pan and cook for another 2 minutes, until wilted.

5

Mix the eggs and cheese together in a bowl. Season well. Preheat the broiler. Pour the egg mixture evenly over the vegetables and cook on low heat for 5–6 minutes. The edges will cook first.

6

Carefully put the pan under the broiler for 5–6 minutes, until the eggs are set and golden. Remove from the heat, leave for 5 minutes, then use a knife to loosen the edges. Turn onto a plate. Slice to serve.

Ask an adult to help you prepare the butternut squash. Be very careful when using a sharp knife. Carefully cut the vegetable into quarters before peeling/cutting the skin off. Then, seed and chop the flesh into chunks.

Pasta and homemade pesto

SERVES 4
PREP 20 MINS
COOK 15 MINS

Nothing beats homemade pesto and its fabulous fresh taste. It's so simple to make and absolutely delicious.

Ingredients

large handful of basil leaves

¼ cup pine nuts, lightly roasted

2 garlic cloves

pinch of sea salt and freshly ground black pepper

3½oz (100g) hard mature cheese, grated

¾ cup extra virgin olive oil

14oz (400g) pasta shapes of your choice

1 Put the basil, pine nuts, garlic, and seasoning in a food processor and blend to form a paste.

Blend it!

2 Add the cheese to the paste and blend again.

3 Slowly drizzle in the oil and blend until the mix forms a sauce consistency. Add more oil if it is too thick.

4 Carefully boil a large pan of water, then add the pasta and cook for 12 minutes, or follow the instructions on the package.

5 Drain the pasta carefully, put it back in the pan, and toss it with the pesto. Serve immediately.

Lentil dhal and paratha bread

This Indian dish is packed with flavor and is not too spicy. The paratha is perfect for dipping in the dhal.

Ingredients

For the paratha bread

¾ cup whole wheat flour

¾ cup all-purpose flour

pinch of sea salt

¼ cup vegetable oil

½ cup rice flour, for dusting

For the dhal

7oz (200g) split red lentils, rinsed and drained

sea salt and freshly ground black pepper

1 tbsp olive oil

1 onion, finely chopped

2 garlic cloves, finely choppe

1 tbsp grated fresh ginger

1 red chile, finely chopped

2 tsp turmeric

14oz (400g) can chopped tomatoes

handful of cilantro, coarsely chopped

lemon wedges, to serve

SERVES 4
PREP 10 MINS
REST 15 MINS
COOK 50 MINS

1

To make the paratha, put the flours and salt in a bowl, make a well in the center, and add 2 tablespoons of olive oil. Mix together with your fingers until combined.

Roll!!

2

Pour in ⅔ cup warm water. Knead to form a dough. Add more water if dry. Roll into a ball, coat in 1 teaspoon of oil. Rest in a bowl, covered with plastic wrap, for 15 minutes.

Knead!

3

Knead the dough for 1 minute, then cut it in half and roll each half into a thick log. Pull 4 pieces from each of the logs. Roll each into a ball, then flatten into a disk.

4

On a surface dusted with rice flour, roll out each disk to 4in (10cm) rounds. Spread a little oil on each round, then fold into quarters. Press and reroll into rounds.

5

Heat a heavy-bottomed frying pan over medium heat. Cook the rounds carefully, one at a time, for 1 minute on each side, until bubbles form. Set aside in a warm place.

6

To make the dhal, add the lentils to a large pan, pour in 3 cups water, season well, and simmer for 20 minutes, until the lentils are soft.

7

Carefully heat the oil in a large frying pan over medium heat. Add the onion. Season well. Cook for 2-3 minutes, until soft. Stir in the garlic, ginger, chile, and turmeric. Cook 2 minutes more.

8

Add in the tomatoes and cook on low heat for 10 minutes, then stir the mix into the cooked red lentils. Add cilantro. Serve with the paratha bread.

Easy
veggie rolls

These crunchy, sweet rolls are a quirky twist on sushi. The vinegar gives the rice its tangy flavor.

Dip your rolls in soy sauce, or even mix it with wasabi, if you like spicy food.

Did you know?

Sushi rice is naturally rich in carbohydrates, but it doesn't contain much fiber. The vegetables add fiber, vitamins, and minerals.

1

Put the rice in a sieve and rinse it under plenty of cold water until the water runs clear.

2

Put the rice in a pan. Add the cold water and carefully bring to a boil, then cover and simmer for 10 minutes.

3

Take the rice off the heat for 10 minutes, still covered. Then put it in a shallow dish. Pour on the vinegar and mix.

Ingredients

4½ oz (125g) sushi rice

¾ cup cold water

1 tsp white balsamic vinegar

1 large cucumber

For the cream cheese filling

6 tbsp cream cheese

¼ cup grated carrot, patted dry with paper towels

½ red or yellow bell pepper, diced

1 tbsp raisins or golden raisins

sea salt and freshly ground black pepper

1 tbsp dark soy sauce

4

Carefully peel 12 thin strips of cucumber. Pat with paper towels to remove excess water.

5

Spread the rice evenly down the center of each strip of cucumber.

To make the filling, mix the cream cheese, carrot, bell pepper, and raisins. Season well.

Add the MIX!

Spoon on small dollops of the cream cheese mix, then roll the cucumber. Do not overfill. Serve with the soy sauce.

Roll it up!

Delicious
drinks

Fruity
freshness

Start your day with an energy-rich protein shake! Whip up the best-ever mango lassi to serve with a spicy dish, or make a rich hot chocolate to warm up on a cold day. Create impressive fizzy fruity drinks to serve at a party.

Shake and stir!

Fruit and nut
shake

This fruity shake has a secret ingredient—tasty almond butter, which boosts the protein and fiber in this delicious drink.

Did you know?

A tablespoon of almond butter contains about 3 grams of protein. It's also a source of iron, fiber, and heart-healthy fats.

1

Place all the ingredients in a blender or food processor.

Ingredients

5½oz (150g) frozen or fresh mixed berries

1 small banana, chopped

1¼ cups almond milk or dairy milk

2 tbsp almond butter

2 tbsp rolled oats

small handful of almonds or cashews

2 Blend until smooth.

Blend!

You can use other fruits, too!

Swap the berries for your favorites.

Kiwis

Pineapples

3

Your shake is best drunk fresh, but can be kept overnight in the fridge.

Mangoes

Fizzy fruit drinks

These cooling drinks look fun and taste amazing!

SERVES 4
PREP 10 MINS

Peach passion

SERVES 4
PREP 10 MINS

Cucumber cooler

SERVES 4-6
PREP 10 MINS

Watermelon fizz

Cucumber cooler

½ cucumber, thinly sliced, plus extra to garnish

2 kiwis, peeled and chopped

1 lime, chopped

handful of mint sprigs, plus extra to garnish

handful of ice cubes

2⅓ cups tonic water

Special equipment

muddler

1 Put most of the cucumber in the bottom of the glasses, then add the kiwi, lime, and mint leaves. Muddle (stir and squash) it all to release the flavors.

2 Add the ice cubes and pour in the tonic water. Garnish with the extra cucumber slices and mint leaves.

Watermelon fizz

1 watermelon, peeled carefully, cut into quarters, seeded and cut into chunks

2 limes, chopped (reserve a few thin slices for garnish)

6 tsp sugar

handful of strawberries, coarsely chopped (reserve a few slices for garnish)

handful of ice cubes

2 cups sparkling water or seltzer

handful of mint sprigs, to garnish

1 Puree the watermelon and limes in a blender until smooth. Pour the sugar onto a plate.

2 Wet the rim of each glass and place on the sugar to coat the rim. Pour the puree into each glass. Add the strawberries, ice, and water. Garnish with mint leaves and reserved slices of lime and strawberry.

Peach passion

a few mint sprigs

juice of 1 lime

1 small fresh pineapple, peeled and coarsely chopped (reserve a few pieces with skin on for garnish)

2 peaches, pitted and chopped

handful of crushed ice

3¾ cups sparkling water

Special equipment

muddler

1 Muddle the mint leaves and lime juice in the glasses. Puree the pineapple in a blender.

2 Put the pineapple, peaches, ice, and sparkling water in the glasses. Garnish with the reserved peach slices.

Oat milk
hot chocolate

SERVES 2
PREP 5 MINS
COOK 10 MINS

This delicious oat milk hot chocolate is the perfect drink for cold days.

Vegan variation

For a dairy-free drink, replace the dark and milk chocolate with 3oz (85g) vegan chocolate chips, and use grated vegan chocolate.

Ingredients

1 cup oat milk

1 cinnamon stick

1¾oz (50g) dark chocolate (70% or above), broken into pieces

1oz (25g) milk chocolate, broken into pieces

handful of grated dark chocolate, to serve

mini vegan marshmallows, to serve

1

Put the oat milk and cinnamon stick in a pan, bring almost to a boil, then carefully remove from the heat. Let cool for 10 minutes. Remove the cinnamon stick.

2

Add both the chocolates to a heatproof bowl and place the bowl on a pan of simmering water. Carefully and gently heat until melted, stirring occasionally.

Stir it!

3

Return the pan of milk to the heat and carefully add the melted chocolate. Whisk until combined. Pour into two cups and top with the grated dark chocolate and marshmallows to serve.

Mango lassi

Lassi is a super-refreshing, smoothie-style drink from India. It's delicious served cold!

Did you know?

Yogurt and milk are both rich in calcium, which is important for strong bones. They also provide a good amount of vitamins B2 and B12.

1

Blend it!

Put the mango, milk, and yogurt into a blender and puree until blended.

Ingredients

2 mangoes, peeled, pitted, and flesh coarsely chopped

¾ cup milk

1¼ cups plain yogurt

handful of ice cubes

2 Add the ice cubes and blend again.

Puree!

You can use other fruits, too!

Swap the mango for your favorites.

Avocados

Peaches

3

Trickle in a little more milk if the lassi is too thick. Pour into glasses to serve.

Strawberries

Enticing
entrées

Stack it up!

Satisfy your appetite with delicious dinners that are all easy to cook. Make these lentil and halloumi burgers for your friends or whip up a curry for your family. The dishes in this section will soon be on your list of favorites.

Sweet potato
lasagna

SERVES 4
PREP 15 MINS
COOK 1 HR 25 MINS

Instead of pasta, this layered lasagna uses delicious sweet potatoes and is filled with a tasty mix of lentils and mushrooms. It's really good for you, too!

1

Preheat the oven to 400°F (200°C). Put the potato in a pan of salted water, carefully bring to a boil, then reduce to simmer and cook for 3 minutes. Drain well.

2

In a large frying pan, heat the oil over medium heat. Carefully add the onion and season well, then cook for 2 minutes. Add the garlic and oregano and cook for a few seconds.

3

Stir in the mushrooms and cook for about 5–6 minutes, until they start to soften and become juicy.

4

Add the tomatoes, 1¾ cups boiling water, and the lentils. Carefully bring to a boil, then reduce the heat to simmer and cook for 15 minutes, until the mixture has thickened.

5

Spoon a third of the lentil mix into an ovenproof dish, layer with sweet potatoes, and spread with some ricotta. Repeat the layering twice more.

6

Top with the grated cheese, cover with foil, and bake in the oven for 50 minutes to an hour. Carefully remove the foil for the last 10 minutes so the top turns golden and bubbly.

Ingredients

4 sweet potatoes, peeled and thinly sliced

1 tbsp olive oil

1 onion, finely chopped

sea salt and freshly ground black pepper

2 garlic cloves, finely chopped

pinch of dried oregano

9oz (250g) chestnut mushrooms, finely chopped

14oz (400g) can chopped tomatoes

14oz (400g) can brown lentils, rinsed and drained

9oz (250g) ricotta cheese

1¾oz (50g) hard cheese, grated

Grate!

Vegetable pot roast

SERVES 4
PREP 15 MINS
COOK 55 MINS

This is a hearty dish of delicious beans, tomatoes, potatoes, and herbs, all thrown into the pot to meld together and work their magic!

1

Carefully heat the oil in a large saucepan over medium heat. Add the onion, season well, and cook for 2 minutes. Add the garlic and cook for another minute, then stir in the paprika.

2

Add the potatoes, tomatoes, and the beans. Mix together.

Toss it all together!

3

Carefully pour in the stock, bring to a boil, then reduce to simmer. Cover and cook the veggies for 45 minutes, until the vegetables are tender.

4

Add the peas, dill, and some more seasoning. Cook for 5 minutes. Carefully transfer to a serving dish and keep warm.

Ingredients

1 tbsp olive oil

1 onion, finely chopped

pinch of sea salt and freshly ground black pepper

2 garlic cloves, finely chopped

2 tsp paprika

9oz (250g) baby new potatoes, larger ones halved

large handful of cherry tomatoes

7oz (200g) green beans, trimmed and halved

1 vegetable stock cube, dissolved in 3 cups hot water

handful of frozen peas, defrosted

handful of dill, chopped

9oz (250g) brown rice, to serve

5

Carefully boil the rice until tender, or follow the package instructions. Drain and serve with the veggie roast.

Did you know?

This meal is high in fiber and provides a good variety of vitamins and minerals. To boost the protein content, serve it with grated cheese.

Sweet potato
falafel balls

MAKES 30
PREP 15 MNS
COOK 50 MINS

Falafel is a Middle Eastern snack that is now popular all over the world. It will soon be a favorite of yours, too.

pita bread

yogurt and mint dip

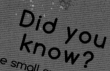

Did you know?

One small sweet potato provides over half your recommended amount of vitamin A, which is important for healthy skin and eyes.

1

Preheat the oven to 400°F (200°C). Prick the sweet potato and place it on a baking sheet. Bake for 40 minutes. Allow to cool slightly. Leave the oven on.

2

chickpeas

ground cumin

smoked paprika

flat-leaf parsley

Place the chickpeas, garlic, spices, parsley, and seasoning in a food processor. Pulse until chopped.

3

Remove the skin and coarsely chop the cooked potato. Add to the food processor with the baking powder, lemon juice, and flour. Pulse until combined.

4

sesame seeds

Shape the mixture into about 30 balls. Coat the balls in sesame seeds and bake for 10 minutes.

Ingredients

1 medium sweet potato, about 9oz (250g)

15oz (420g) can chickpeas, well rinsed and drained

1 garlic clove, crushed

1 tsp ground cumin

2 tsp ground cilantro

1 tsp smoked paprika

2 tbsp chopped flat-leaf parsley

1 tsp salt

1 tsp freshly ground black pepper

1 tsp baking powder

2 tsp lemon juice

2 tbsp all-purpose flour

¼ cup sesame seeds

pita bread, to serve

green salad, to serve

For the yogurt and mint dip

½ cup low-fat plain yogurt

2 tbsp chopped fresh mint

¼ cucumber, finely chopped

5

Mix it!

yogurt

cucumber

fresh mint

Mix the ingredients for the dip. Serve the falafel with warmed pita, salad, and dip.

Pizza dough

Once you have mastered this simple pizza dough and sauce, turn to page 94 and choose a tasty topping!

MAKES 4 PIZZAS
PREP 20 MINS
RISE $1^1/_2$ HRS

Ingredients

3 cups bread flour, plus extra for dusting

pinch of sea salt

$^1/_4$oz (7g) package dried yeast

3 tbsp olive oil, plus extra for greasing

1

Using a stand mixer, put the flour, salt, and yeast into the mixer bowl. Attach the dough hook and mix on slow speed. Add the oil and slowly pour in 1¼ cups lukewarm water.

2

Keep mixing slowly until the dough comes together. Turn the mixer to a higher speed and mix for 5 minutes, until it forms a ball and slaps against the sides of the bowl.

3

On a lightly floured surface, knead the dough, stretching and pulling as you go. Add flour if sticky, but don't make the dough too dry. Knead for about 10 minutes, or until the dough starts to feel smooth and springy.

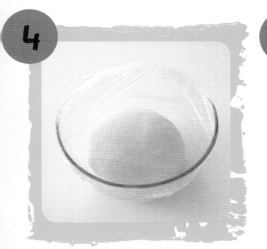

4

Lightly grease a bowl with olive oil, then add the dough. Cover with plastic wrap and put the bowl in a warm place. Leave it to proof for about 1 hour, or until doubled in size.

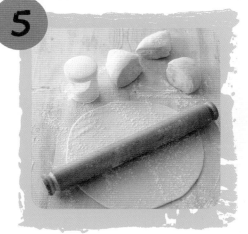

5

Punch the dough down lightly, place it on a floured surface, and cut into four pieces. Cover with plastic wrap and leave for 30 minutes, until it is doubled in size. Then roll it out into a circle.

Once you've made your pizza dough into a ball and it has risen fully (Step 4), you can freeze it. Wrap well in plastic wrap and keep in the freezer for up to one month. When ready to use, defrost in the fridge overnight, then put it in a warm place for an hour to double in size again, before moving to Step 5.

For the pizza sauce, carefully heat 1 tablespoon olive oil in a large frying pan over medium heat. Add 1 onion, finely chopped, and 2 garlic cloves, finely chopped. Season well. Cook for 2 minutes.

Add 2 x 14oz (400g) cans plum tomatoes, cook for 5 minutes, and crush the tomatoes using the back of a wooden spoon. Stir in 2 teaspoons tomato puree and simmer for 10–15 minutes, until the mixture thickens. Add a pinch of dried oregano if you like.

Three ways
with pizza

EACH RECIPE
MAKES 1 PIZZA
PREP 5 MINS
COOK 15 MINS

Now that you've made your pizza dough and tomato sauce, it's time to top the crusts with some delicious veggies!

To prepare a pizza crust, put one ball of dough on a lightly floured surface and roll it gently with a rolling pin, rotating as you go; it will keep springing back. Continue to roll and stretch the dough until you have a large, round circle.

Pizza bianca

Preheat the oven to 425°F (220°C). Put the spinach in a bowl, cover with plastic wrap, and microwave for 1–2 minutes, until it wilts. Squeeze out the water. Carefully put a pizza crust on a hot baking sheet, brush with olive oil, sprinkle with sea salt, and top with the spinach, leaving a ¾in (2cm) edge all around. Scatter with garlic slices and ricotta. Drizzle with a little more oil, then sprinkle with black pepper and chile flakes (if using). Bake in the oven for 10–15 minutes, until the edge of the crust is crispy and the top is bubbling.

Mushrooms and zucchini ribbons

Preheat the oven to 425°F (220°C). Carefully put a pizza crust on a hot baking sheet and spread with tomato sauce, leaving a ¾in (2cm) edge all around. Add the zucchini ribbons and mushrooms, then scatter the grated cheese over the top. Finish with a drizzle of oil and a sprinkling of black pepper. Bake in the oven for 10–15 minutes, until the crust is crispy and the top is bubbling.

Ingredients

Pizza bianca (to top 1 pizza)

2 large handfuls of spinach leaves

extra virgin olive oil, plus extra for topping

pinch of sea salt

2 garlic cloves, thinly sliced

3–4 tbsp ricotta cheese

freshly ground black pepper

sprinkle of chile flakes (optional)

Pesto and sun-dried tomatoes (to top 1 pizza)

3 tbsp tomato sauce

2 tbsp pesto

6 sun-dried tomatoes, chopped

½ ball mozzarella, torn into small pieces

extra virgin olive oil

freshly grated black pepper

Mushrooms and zucchini ribbons (to top 1 pizza)

3 tbsp tomato sauce

1 medium zucchini, thinly sliced into ribbon strips with a peeler

handful of mushrooms, thinly sliced

4½oz (125g) grated mozzarella

extra virgin olive oil

freshly ground black pepper

Pesto and sun-dried tomatoes

Preheat the oven to 425°F (220°C). Carefully put a pizza crust on a hot baking sheet and spread with tomato sauce, leaving a ¾in (2cm) edge all around. Spoon dollops of pesto on top, then scatter with sun-dried tomatoes and mozzarella. Add a sprinkling of black pepper. Bake in the oven for 10–15 minutes, until the crust is crispy and the top is bubbling.

Calzone

A calzone is a folded pizza that is stuffed with a delicious filling. It's important not to add too much filling or it will ooze out.

MAKES 4
PREP 20 MINS
RISE 2$\frac{1}{2}$ HRS
COOK 20 MINS

Ingredients

1 tbsp olive oil, plus extra for greasing

7oz (200g) mushrooms, sliced

pinch of sea salt and freshly ground black pepper

10oz (300g) spinach leaves, torn

$\frac{1}{4}$ cup tomato sauce

7oz (200g) mozzarella

For the dough

4 cups bread flour, plus extra for dusting

$\frac{1}{4}$oz (7g) package dried yeast

pinch of sea salt

1 tbsp olive oil

salad leaves, to serve

1

Put the flour, yeast, and salt into the bowl of a stand mixer. Mix using the dough hook. Add 1¼ cups warm water and the oil. Continue mixing quickly for 10 minutes, until the dough slaps against the sides of the bowl.

2

Using floured hands, scoop the dough out of the bowl and put it onto a lightly floured surface. Knead for 5 minutes.

3

Lightly grease a clean bowl. Put the dough in it and cover with plastic wrap. Let the dough rise in a warm place for 2 hours, or until doubled in size. Preheat the oven to 400°F (200°C).

4

Knock the air out of the dough by gently punching it. Place on a lightly floured surface. Knead for 1 minute, then divide into four balls. Place on a baking sheet and set in a warm place to rise for 30 minutes.

5

Carefully heat the olive oil in a large frying pan over medium heat, then add the mushrooms. Season well. Cook for 2 minutes, until the mushrooms are soft. Stir in the spinach.

6

Put a baking sheet in the oven to warm it. Roll the dough balls out to 8in (20cm) rounds. Spread tomato sauce over the dough circles, leaving a ¾in (2cm) edge all around.

7

Put some mushroom and spinach mixture on half of each round. Sprinkle the mozzarella on top. Wet the edge of the dough with water, then fold over. Pinch the edges to seal. Carefully place on a baking sheet and bake in the oven for 20 minutes. Do this in two batches. Serve with salad leaves.

Spread it!

Veggie sausages and
mashed potatoes

It is really satisfying and fun to make
your own veggie sausages for dinner.
Serve with creamy mashed potatoes,
tasty greens, and a vegetarian gravy.

SERVES 6
PREP 15 MINS
CHILL 50 MINS
COOK 50 MINS

Did you know?
This meal provides plenty of
protein from the lentils, nuts,
and eggs, as well as carbs
from the potatoes and
bread crumbs. For a
balanced meal, all you need
to add is a vegeatble.

1

Soak the mushrooms in a bowl of hot water for 20 minutes. Carefully remove them using a slotted spoon and chop the mushrooms. Reserve the water.

2

Heat half a tablespoon of the oil in a large frying pan over medium heat. Add the onion. Season well. Cook for 3 minutes. Stir in the garlic and cook for 1 minute.

3

Use a food processor to blend the mushrooms, lentils, nuts, apple, bread crumbs, herbs, tomato paste, onion, and garlic into a coarse mixture.

Ingredients

½oz (15g) dried porcini mushrooms

3 tbsp olive oil, for frying

1 onion, finely chopped

sea salt and freshly ground black pepper

2 garlic cloves, finely chopped

2 x 15oz (420g) cans green lentils, rinsed and drained

7oz (200g) ground pecans or walnuts

1 apple, grated

2 cups fresh bread crumbs

handful of thyme leaves

handful of flat-leaf parsley, finely chopped

½ tbsp tomato paste

2 eggs

4 tsp vegetarian gravy granules, dissolved in 1¼ cups boiling water, to serve

10oz (300g) broccoli, steamed, to serve

For the mashed potatoes

1lb 2oz (500g) potatoes, peeled and chopped

2 tbsp butter

⅔ cup milk

4

Crack in one egg at a time. Blend again. Add a little of the reserved mushroom soaking water. Season well. Put the mixture into a bowl. Chill for 30 minutes.

5

Make 10–12 balls. Squish them, using your hands. Then roll them into sausage shapes. Put them on a plate or baking sheet. Chill for 20 minutes.

6

Over medium heat, fry the sausages in the remaining oil until golden. Turn them regularly. Carefully boil the potatoes until soft. Drain and then mash the potatoes. Stir in the butter and milk.

Mash it!

99

Cauliflower
steaks

This is an unusual and tasty way to cook cauliflower. It is so delicious, you'll end up eating lots of this healthy "steak."

Did you know?
Cauliflower is a good source of vitamin K, which will help keep your bones healthy and strong.

Ingredients

2 large heads cauliflower, outer leaves removed

3 tbsp olive oil

sea salt and freshly ground black pepper

2 tsp turmeric

grated zest of 1 lemon

1 red chile, seeded and finely chopped

handful of flat-leaf parsley, leaves only, finely chopped

3 tsp capers, chopped

6 potatoes, peeled and cubed, to serve

2–3 rosemary sprigs, leaves removed, to serve

1 Chop!

Place the heads of cauliflower on a board with the stems facing up, then carefully slice vertically into even-sized steaks. You should get 3–4 per cauliflower. Use all the smaller pieces around the edges, too.

2

Mix 2 tablespoons of the oil, some seasoning, the turmeric, lemon zest, and half the chile in a medium bowl. Use a pastry brush to coat all of the cauliflower steaks with the mixture.

3

Carefully heat a grill pan to hot, then add the cauliflower. In batches, cook the steaks for 4–5 minutes, then turn over and cook for another 4–5 minutes, or until the cauliflower is charred and just tender.

4

Put the steaks on serving plates, and scatter parsley, capers, and the remaining chile over the top before serving.

Serve with...

Preheat the oven to 400°F (200°C). Put the potatoes and rosemary in a large roasting pan. Drizzle the remaining oil on top and season well. Use your hands to coat the potatoes and to spread them out in the pan. Roast for 25–30 minutes, or until tender.

Broccoli and bean
stir-fry

This tasty dish is really easy to make and is perfect for a quick dinner on busy weeknights.

Did you know?
Broccoli and tomatoes are both rich in vitamin C, which will help your body absorb the iron from the beans.

Ingredients

1 head broccoli, cut into florets

7oz (200g) thin green beans, trimmed and chopped into thirds

1 tbsp sesame oil

bunch of scallions, trimmed and thinly sliced (reserve some of the green ends for topping)

2 garlic cloves, thinly sliced

1 red chile, halved, seeded, and thinly sliced

1 tbsp fresh ginger, peeled and thinly sliced

14oz (400g) can kidney beans, rinsed and drained

handful of cherry tomatoes

¼oz (10g) black or white sesame seeds, or a mixture of both

10oz (300g) fresh, not dried, medium noodles

handful of cilantro (optional)

For the sauce

3 tbsp lime juice

2 tbsp light soy sauce, plus extra if needed

2 tsp granulated sugar

2 tsp cornstarch

1

Carefully put the broccoli in a pan of boiling, salted water and cook for 5 minutes. Add the green beans for the last 3 minutes. Drain, using a colander, then submerge them in a bowl of cold water. Drain again when ready to use.

2

Carefully heat the sesame oil in a large wok over high heat. Be careful near hot oil and a hot wok. Add the white scallions and some of the greens and cook for 1 minute. Add the garlic, chile, and ginger. Cook for 1 minute more. Stir continuously, so the stir-fry doesn't burn.

Put the drained broccoli and green beans in the wok. Add the beans and tomatoes. Stir and cook for 2 minutes. Add the sauce mixture (see below) and let it bubble for 2 minutes, stirring continuously.

3

Mix it!

Put the sauce ingredients to a small bowl and whisk together, ready to add to the wok.

4

Add the noodles and stir so they are very well coated and heated through. Sprinkle with the remaining green scallions, sesame seeds, and cilantro, if using. Serve while piping hot.

Chickpea and sweet potato
curry

This isn't a hot curry, although you can ramp it up with more chiles if you like. The meal is a fantastic mixture of flavors and colors.

SERVES 4
PREP 10 MINS
COOK 50 MINS

Ingredients

1 tbsp olive oil

1 red onion, coarsely chopped

sea salt and freshly ground black pepper

2 garlic cloves, finely chopped

1 red chile, seeded and finely chopped

1 tbsp fresh ginger, grated

2 tsp garam masala

2 sweet potatoes, peeled and cubed

14oz (400g) can chickpeas, rinsed and drained

14oz (400g) can chopped tomatoes

14oz (400g) can coconut milk

10oz (300g) spinach leaves

bunch of cilantro, chopped

7oz (200g) brown basmati rice, to serve

For the salad

1 tomato, coarsely chopped

½ cucumber, coarsely chopped

½ red onion, coarsely chopped

handful of cilantro leaves, chopped

1

Carefully heat the oil in a large pan over medium heat, then add the onion. Season well and cook for 2–3 minutes, until soft. Stir in the garlic, chile, ginger, and garam masala, and cook for 1 minute more. Add the sweet potatoes and stir.

2

Carefully add the chickpeas, tomatoes, and coconut milk and bring to a boil. Then reduce to simmer and cook gently for 15 minutes, until the potatoes are tender.

3

Add the spinach leaves a little at a time, stir, and cook until they wilt. Then stir in the cilantro.

Serve with...

Put the rice in a sieve and rinse. Bring 1¾ cups water to a boil in a large pan. Carefully add the rice to the boiling water. Cook for 25–30 minutes, or until tender. All the water should be absorbed by the rice. In a small bowl, mix the ingredients together for the side salad.

Coconut rice with spicy beans

These colorful veggies look great and taste amazing. It's a really quick dinner to make.

SERVES 4
PREP 10 MINS
COOK 20 MINS

Spicy!

To make this dish vegan, swap the honey for maple syrup.

1

Carefully heat the sesame oil in a large frying pan over medium heat. Add the scallions and bell peppers and stir for 3 minutes. Add the ginger, chile, chile flakes, and lime zest.

2

Stir in the lime juice, soy sauce mix, and season with black pepper. Stir for 2 minutes.

Stir it well.

3

Add the red kidney beans and sugarsnap peas. Stir well to coat and heat through. Drizzle the hot chile sauce over the top (if using). Keep hot.

Ingredients

1 tbsp sesame oil

bunch of scallions, thinly sliced

2 red bell peppers, halved, seeded, and coarsely chopped

1 tbsp fresh ginger, grated

1 red chile, thinly sliced

sprinkle of chile flakes

grated zest and juice of 1 lime

2 tbsp dark soy sauce, mixed with 2 tsp honey

freshly ground black pepper

14oz (400g) can red kidney beans, rinsed and drained

handful of sugarsnap peas, sliced diagonally

hot chile sauce, to serve (optional)

7oz (200g) basmati rice, rinsed

¾ cup coconut milk

4

To make the coconut rice, put the rice in a pan and pour in the coconut milk and ¾ cup water. Add a pinch of salt and carefully bring to a boil, then cover and reduce to simmer. Cook for 15 minutes, until the rice is tender and the liquid has been absorbed. Serve with the spicy beans.

Veggie goulash with herb dumplings

Spiced with sweet paprika and packed with delicious vegetables, this veggie goulash is made extra special with the herb dumplings.

Ingredients

1 tbsp olive oil

1 onion, finely chopped

sea salt and freshly ground black pepper

2 garlic cloves, finely chopped

4 carrots, peeled and diced

2 red bell peppers, halved, seeded, and coarsely chopped

4 potatoes, peeled and cut into chunks

4 tomatoes, coarsely chopped

1 tbsp sweet paprika

14oz (400g) can mixed beans or butter beans, rinsed and drained

1 vegetable stock cube, dissolved in 3 cups hot water

few sprigs of flat-leaf parsley, finely chopped

For the dumplings

⅔ cup self-rising flour

pinch of sea salt

4 tbsp butter, cubed

a few chives, snipped

SERVES 6
PREP 20 MINS
COOK 1½ HRS

These tempting treats contain fruits and vegetables, which add delicious flavor and texture. Roll up chocolate energy balls, mix up tasty orange cookies, make your own avocado ice cream, then bake beet brownies and zingy lime pie.

Almond, chocolate, and coconut
energy balls

These are so easy to make and require no cooking: just mix, roll, and chill! They'll give you instant energy when hunger strikes.

MAKES 12
PREP 15 MINS
CHILL 20 MINS
OR OVERNIGHT

Mix it!

raisins

cocoa powder

honey

shredded coconut

hot water

Ingredients

¾ cup whole almonds, skin on

3 tbsp dark chocolate cocoa powder

½ cup raisins

⅓ cup shredded, unsweetened coconut

1 tsp honey

⅔ cup shredded, unsweetened coconut, to roll the balls in

1 Put the almonds in a food processor and pulse until finely chopped. Add the cocoa, raisins, and ⅓ cup coconut and blend again. Add the honey and carefully pour in about 2 tablespoons hot (not boiling) water. Puree until the mixture comes together.

ROLL IT UP!

2 Roll the mixture into 12 balls. Put the ⅔ cup coconut in a small bowl. Roll half of the balls in the coconut. Put all the balls on a baking sheet lined with wax paper. Chill for 20 minutes, or overnight.

Vegan variation

Swap the honey with maple syrup or agave nectar to make these energy balls vegan.

3 Put the balls in an airtight container and eat them when you need an energy boost. Alternatively, they are great in gift boxes.

115

Avocado and banana
ice cream

Surprise your friends with this vegan ice cream, which is created without an ice-cream maker.

MAKES **1 QUART**
PREP **15 MINS**
PLUS CHURNING AND
FREEZING TIME

1

In a food processor, add the coconut milk, avocados, banana, matcha tea, lime juice, maple syrup, and peppermint extract. Puree until blended and smooth. Taste for sweetness and stir in more maple syrup if needed.

2

Transfer to a freezer-proof container and put the container in the freezer for about 1 hour.

3

Remove the container from the freezer and put the mixture back in the food processor. Blend again until smooth. Pour it back into the container and place in the freezer.

4

Take the ice cream out and blend again after 20 minutes, so it doesn't get too frozen. This helps keep it from becoming crystallized and it remains creamy. Do this a couple more times, so the ice cream becomes nice and thick.

5

On the last time in the food processor, blend, then stir in the chocolate chips. Put the ice cream back into the container and return to the freezer. Serve when frozen.

Ingredients

2 x 14oz (400g) cans coconut milk

3 ripe avocados, pitted

2 ripe bananas

½ tsp matcha green tea powder

juice of 1 lime (to prevent discoloration)

3 tbsp maple syrup

2 drops of peppermint extract

2½oz (75g) vegan dark chocolate chips (70% cocoa) or chocolate broken into small pieces

Orange and chocolate
cookies

When you get the hang of this easy cookie dough mix, you can become more adventurous and add your favorite spices or flavored chocolate.

SERVES 8
PREP 20 MINS
COOK 10 MINS

1

Preheat the oven to 350°F (180°C). Grease 2 baking sheets. Pour the flour into a large bowl, add the butter, and rub it in using your fingertips, until the mixture looks like bread crumbs.

2

Stir it!

Add the sugar and rub it in. Stir in the orange zest and the white chocolate chips.

Grate it!

3

Using your hands, bring the dough together. Use a little more flour if the dough is too wet. Halve the dough and roll both halves into a sausage shape. Cut each shape into 8 pieces.

4

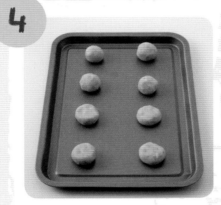

Roll the dough pieces into 16 balls. Put them on 2 greased baking sheets and gently press down on each one. Bake in the oven for 10 minutes, or until golden.

Ingredients

¾ cup self-rising flour

7 tbsp unsalted butter, chilled, cut into cubes, plus extra for greasing

¼ cup granulated sugar

grated zest of 1 orange

2oz (60g) white chocolate chips

5

Leave the cookies on the sheet to cool a little, then carefully transfer the cookies to a wire rack to cool fully.

Cool it!

Beet brownies

These are good and fudgy, as brownies should be. The grated beets keep them moist and make them a little bit healthier.

MAKES 12
PREP 20 MINS
COOK 1 HOUR

Top tip
Put the brownies in an airtight container and they will keep for 3–4 days.

Top tip

It's a good idea to wear rubber gloves while you grate the beets, as the process can be messy and stain your hands purple!

1 Grate!

Preheat the oven to 350°F (180°C). Carefully add the beets to a saucepan of boiling water. Then reduce the heat to simmer, cover, and cook for 30–35 minutes, until tender. Drain well. When cool enough to handle, peel, grate, and set aside.

In a heatproof bowl, add the chocolate and butter, place the bowl over a pan of simmering water, and carefully heat until melted. Stir well. Remove from the heat and set aside.

3

Add the sugar and eggs to a bowl and whisk until well combined, then mix together with the chocolate.

Ingredients

9oz (250g) raw beets

7oz (200g) dark chocolate, broken into even pieces

14 tbsp unsalted butter, cubed, plus extra for greasing

¾ cup granulated sugar

3 eggs

1 cup self-rising flour

½ cup dark chocolate cocoa powder

Special equipment

8½in (22cm) square baking pan, 1½in (4cm) deep, greased

4

Stir in the flour and cocoa, then stir in the grated beets until mixed well.

5

Pour the mixture into the pan, smooth the top, and bake for 25 minutes. Poke a skewer into the brownies to test that they are cooked. Carefully remove from the oven and leave in the pan to cool, then remove and slice into squares.

Zingy lime pie

This delicious dessert is fun to make. It's sweet, sour, and crunchy!

SERVES 6
PREP 20 MINS
COOK 25 MINS
PLUS CHILLING

1

Preheat the oven to 350°F (180°C). Pulse the crackers in a food processor until they look like bread crumbs. Melt the butter in a saucepan. Tip in the crackers and mix well with the butter.

Mix it!

Ingredients

7oz (200g) graham crackers

4 tbsp unsalted butter

For the filling

3 large egg yolks

grated zest of 2 limes and juice of 4 limes

1½ cups sweetened condensed milk

¾ cup heavy cream, for the topping

Special equipment

8½in (22cm) fluted pie pan

piping bag

* Please note: the finished recipe contains egg that isn't fully cooked.

2

Pour the graham cracker mix into the pie dish and spread evenly. Press firmly into the bottom and sides. Bake in the oven for 10 minutes. Remove and cool.

3

In a large bowl, beat the egg yolks for 1 minute. Add the lime zest, juice, and the condensed milk. Beat again until well combined.

4

Pour the filling over the crust, smooth the top, and bake for 15 minutes, or until just set. Remove from the oven and let cool completely. Chill the fridge until ready to serve.

5

To decorate, beat the cream in a bowl until it just starts to form soft peaks. Put the cream in the piping bag and pipe around the edges of the pie.

Decorate it!

Nutrition
information

Check here to find out what's in your food. The numbers don't include extras or variations suggested in the recipes. Remember to eat a balanced diet.

Best breakfasts

Avocado on sourdough toast
- Fat 23g
- Saturated fat 4.5g
- Protein 10.5g
- Fiber 7g
- Salt 1.3g

Crunchy, sweet pancakes
- Fat 4g
- Saturated fat 1g
- Protein 4g
- Fiber 1g
- Salt 0.4g

Scrambled eggs
- Fat 27g
- Saturated fat 15g
- Protein 9g
- Fiber 0g
- Salt 1.2g

Swiss oatmeal
- Fat 12g
- Saturated fat 4g
- Protein 10g
- Fiber 5g
- Salt 0.2g

Mango yogurt with toast dippers
- Fat 15.5g
- Saturated fat 9g
- Protein 10g
- Fiber 5g
- Salt 0.5g

Poached eggs with greens and hollandaise sauce
- Fat 64g
- Saturated fat 35g
- Protein 18g
- Fiber 4.5g
- Salt 2.3g

Super snacks

Flatbreads and dips
- Fat 35g
- Saturated fat 6g
- Protein 16g
- Fiber 8g
- Salt 1.3g

Crudités and dips
- Fat 22g
- Saturated fat 14g
- Protein 11g
- Fiber 3.5g
- Salt 1.5g

Plantain chips and dips
- Fat 24g
- Saturated fat 5g
- Protein 4g
- Fiber 1g
- Salt 0.9g

Homemade nachos
- Fat 30g
- Saturated fat 14g
- Protein 23g
- Fiber 8.5g
- Salt 1.8g

Warm and fruity bulgur wheat salad
- Fat 16.5g
- Saturated fat 2.5g
- Protein 16g
- Fiber 10g
- Salt 0.3g

Cheese and herb muffins
- Fat 9g
- Saturated fat 5g
- Protein 7g
- Fiber 0.5g
- Salt 0.6g

Summer rolls (per roll)
- Fat 0.5g
- Saturated fat 0g
- Protein 1.5g
- Fiber 0.5g
- Salt 0.6g

Watermelon and feta summer salad
- Fat 16g
- Saturated fat 6g
- Protein 14.5g
- Fiber 3.5g
- Salt 0.9g

Parsnip and sweet potato fries
- Fat 7g
- Saturated fat 1g
- Protein 3g
- Fiber 8g
- Salt 0.4g

Lovely lunches

Pumpkin soup
- Fat 6.5g
- Saturated fat 1.5g
- Protein 8g
- Fiber 5g
- Salt 0.7g

Vegetable wraps
- Fat 38g
- Saturated fat 14g
- Protein 18g
- Fiber 6g
- Salt 2.9g

Vegetable frittata
- Fat 16g
- Saturated fat 5.5g
- Protein 17g
- Fiber 3g
- Salt 0.9g

Pearl barley risotto
- Fat 14g
- Saturated fat 3g
- Protein 13.5g
- Fiber 5g
- Salt 0.6g

Pasta and homemade pesto
- Fat 51g
- Saturated fat 10.5g
- Protein 21g
- Fiber 4g
- Salt 0.4g

Quesadillas
- Fat 16g
- Saturated fat 4.5g
- Protein 15g
- Fiber 9g
- Salt 1.3g

Lentil dhal and paratha bread
- Fat 16g
- Saturated fat 1.5g
- Protein 21g
- Fiber 7.5g
- Salt 0.6g

Veggie gyoza (per gyoza)
- Fat 0.5g
- Saturated fat 0.1g
- Protein 2g
- Fiber 0.1g
- Salt 0.4g

Easy veggie rolls (per roll)
- Fat 2g
- Saturated fat 1g
- Protein 1.5g
- Fiber 0.7g
- Salt 0.25g

Delicious drinks

Fruit and nut shake (2 servings)
- Fat 20g
- Saturated fat 2g
- Protein 10g
- Fiber 4.5g
- Salt 0.2g

Peach passion
- Fat 0g
- Saturated fat 0g
- Protein 0g
- Fiber 3g
- Salt 0g

Cucumber cooler
- Fat 0g
- Saturated fat 0g
- Protein 0.5g
- Fiber 1g
- Salt 0g

Oat milk hot chocolate
- Fat 18.5g
- Saturated fat 9.5g
- Protein 4g
- Fiber 3.5g
- Salt 0.3g

Watermelon fizz
- Fat 0g
- Saturated fat 0g
- Protein 0g
- Fiber 0g
- Salt 0g

Mango lassi
- Fat 4g
- Saturated fat 3g
- Protein 6.5g
- Fiber 2g
- Salt 0.2g

Sweet potato lasagna

- Fat 15g
- Saturated fat 8g
- Protein 18g
- Fiber 9g
- Salt 0.9g

Vegetable pot roast

- Fat 6g
- Saturated fat 1g
- Protein 10g
- Fiber 5g
- Salt 0.3g

Sweet potato falafel balls

- Fat 15.5g
- Saturated fat 2.5g
- Protein 10g
- Fiber 6.5g
- Salt 1.6g

Mushroom and zucchini ribbons pizza

- Fat 68g
- Saturated fat 31g
- Protein 50g
- Fiber 5.5g
- Salt 3.5g

Enticing entrées

Pizza bianca

- Fat 31g
- Saturated fat 8g
- Protein 25g
- Fiber 6.5g
- Salt 2.2g

Pesto and sun-dried tomatoes pizza

- Fat 60g
- Saturated fat 20g
- Protein 41g
- Fiber 5g
- Salt 2.9g

Calzone

- Fat 18g
- Saturated fat 8.5g
- Protein 24g
- Fiber 6g
- Salt 1.1g

Veggie sausages and mashed potatoes

- Fat 21.5g
- Saturated fat 3.5g
- Protein 10g
- Fiber 4g
- Salt 0.2g

Cauliflower steaks

- Fat 10g
- Saturated fat 1.5g
- Protein 15g
- Fiber 9g
- Salt 0.6g

Broccoli and bean stir-fry

- Fat 7g
- Saturated fat 1g
- Protein 10.5g
- Fiber 7g
- Salt 1.3g

Chickpea and sweet potato curry

- Fat 21g
- Saturated fat 15g
- Protein 11g
- Fiber 8g
- Salt 0.4g

Coconut rice with spicy beans

- Fat 12g
- Saturated fat 8g
- Protein 10g
- Fiber 6g
- Salt 1g

Veggie goulash with herb dumplings

- Fat 10.5g
- Saturated fat 5g
- Protein 9g
- Fiber 6g
- Salt 0.6g

Lentil burgers with halloumi

- Fat 8g
- Saturated fat 3g
- Protein 17g
- Fiber 7g
- Salt 1.5g

Sweet stuff

Almond, chocolate, and coconut energy balls

- Fat 7g
- Saturated fat 3g
- Protein 2g
- Fiber 1.5g
- Salt 0g

Avocado and banana ice cream, ½ cup (100ml)

- Fat 19g
- Saturated fat 13.5g
- Protein 2g
- Fiber 1g
- Salt 0g

Orange and chocolate cookies

- Fat 11.5g
- Saturated fat 7g
- Protein 2g
- Fiber 0.5g
- Salt 0.15g

Beet brownies

- Fat 19.5g
- Saturated fat 12g
- Protein 5g
- Fiber 1.5g
- Salt 0.22g

Zingy lime pie

- Fat 40g
- Saturated fat 22g
- Protein 9g
- Fiber 0.5g
- Salt 0.7g

Glossary

amino acids organic molecules used by living organisms to make proteins.

aromatic a pleasant or spicy smell.

batter a thin liquid used to make light cakes and pancakes.

beat stirring or mixing quickly until smooth, using a whisk, spoon, or mixer.

blend mixing ingredients together in a blender or food processor until combined

boil heating liquid in a pan over high heat so that it bubbles strongly.

chill cooling food in a fridge.

combine mixing ingredients together evenly.

consistency how runny or thick a mixture is.

dice cutting an ingredient into small, equal cubes.

dissolve melting or liquifying a substance (often sugar in water).

dough the mixture of flour, water, sugar, and salt before it is baked into bread.

drain removing excess liquid from food, often in a colander.

drizzle pouring slowly, in a trickle.

enzymes proteins made from amino acids that spark off chemical reactions in the body, such as breaking down lactose in milk.

fold mixing ingredients together gently to keep the air in the mixture.

fry cooking food in oil.

grate shredding an ingredient into little pieces by rubbing it on a grater.

grease rubbing butter or oil onto a baking sheet or pan to stop food from sticking.

juice squeezing liquid out of a fruit or vegetable.

knead pressing and folding dough with your hands until it is smooth and stretchy. This distributes the yeast.

line placing parchment paper or foil in a pan or on a baking sheet so that food won't stick to it.

lukewarm mildly warm.

mash crushing ingredients with a fork or potato masher.

melt heating a solid substance until it becomes a liquid.

mix combining ingredients together, either by hand or with equipment.

moist slightly wet.

muddle squashing and stirring ingredients to release their flavors.

peaks raised areas, for instance, with whipped cream, that look like the tops of mountains.

phytochemical a chemical compound made by plants.

pipe making a strip of frosting as a decoration on a cake or cupcake.

pit removing the pit from fruits or vegetables.

preheat turning the oven on and heating it to the correct temperature before baking food in it.

process blending an ingredient or ingredients in a food processor.

proofing the final rise of bread dough before baking.

pungent a strong, sharp taste or smell.

puree blending fruits or vegetables in a blender to make a thick pulp.

ripe when a fruit is soft and ready to be eaten.

rise dough gets bigger in size when left in a warm place.

roll out flattening out and shaping dough or pastry using a rolling pin.

rub in rubbing flour and butter together with your fingers to create a texture that looks like bread crumbs.

season adding salt and freshly ground black pepper to a dish to add flavor.

serving an amount or helping of food.

set leaving food on the work surface, in the fridge, or in the freezer until it firms up and turns solid.

sift using a sieve to remove lumps from dry ingredients.

simmer cooking a liquid over low heat so that it is bubbling gently.

slice using a knife to cut food into strips.

sprinkle scattering a food lightly over another food.

transfer moving something from one place to another.

well a dip made in flour in which to crack an egg or pour liquid into.

whisk evenly mixing ingredients together with a whisk.

yeast a type of fungus that when added to flour, water, and salt causes the mixture to rise.

zest the skin of a citrus fruit that has been grated with a grater or a zester.

Index

Acknowledgments

DORLING KINDERSLEY would like to thank the following people for their assistance in the preparation of this book: Anne Damerell for legal assistance; Laura Nickoll for proofreading; Helen Peters for compiling the index; Annabel Hartog for recipe testing; Carrie Love and Rachael Parfitt Hunt for photo shoot prop styling; Eleanor Bates, Rachael Hare, Becky Walsh, James King, Clare Lloyd, Abi Luscombe, Charlotte Milner, and Seeta Parmar for assistance at photo shoots.

The publisher would also like to thank the following for their kind permission to reproduce their photographs: (Key: a-above; b-below/bottom; c-center; f-far; l-left; r-right; t-top)

6 Dreamstime.com: Ljupcho Jovkovski (clb) Cover images: Front: 123RF.com: Jessmine ca; Dreamstime.com: Primopiano (Background); Back: Dreamstime.com: Primopiano (Background)